D0820173

The
Importance of
**SCIENTIFIC
THEORY**

The Importance of
Evolution Theory

Stephen Currie

ReferencePoint
Press®

San Diego, CA

© 2016 ReferencePoint Press, Inc.
Printed in the United States

For more information, contact:
ReferencePoint Press, Inc.
PO Box 27779
San Diego, CA 92198
www.ReferencePointPress.com

LIBRARY OF CONGRESS CATALOGING-IN-PUBLICATION DATA

Currie, Stephen, 1960-
  The importance of evolution theory / by Stephen Currie.
    pages cm. -- (The importance of scientific theory)
  Includes bibliographical references and index.
  Audience: Grades 9 to 12.
  ISBN-13: 978-1-60152-896-4 (hardback)
  ISBN-10: 1-60152-896-5 (hardback)
  1. Evolution (Biology)--Juvenile literature. 2. Evolution (Biology)--Social aspects--Juvenile
literature. I. Title.
  QH367.1C87 2015
  576.8--dc23
                                                              2015005636

CONTENTS

What is the nature of science? The authors of "Understanding the Scientific Enterprise: The Nature of Science in the Next Generation Science Standards," answer that question this way: "Science is a way of explaining the natural world. In common parlance, science is both a set of practices and the historical accumulation of knowledge. An essential part of science education is learning science and engineering practices and developing knowledge of the concepts that are foundational to science disciplines. Further, students should develop an understanding of the enterprise of science as a whole—the wondering, investigating, questioning, data collecting and analyzing."

Examples from history offer a valuable way to explore the nature of science and understand the core ideas and concepts around which all life revolves. When English chemist John Dalton formulated a theory in 1803 that all matter consists of small, indivisible particles called atoms and that atoms of different elements have different properties, he was building on the ideas of earlier scientists as well as relying on his own experimentation, observation, and analysis. His atomic theory, which also proposed that atoms cannot be created or destroyed, was not entirely accurate, yet his ideas are remarkably close to the modern understanding of atoms. Intrigued by his findings, other scientists continued to test and build on Dalton's ideas until eventually—a century later—actual proof of the atom's existence emerged.

The story of these discoveries and what grew from them is presented in *The Importance of Atomic Theory*, one volume in ReferencePoint's series *The Importance of Scientific Theory*. The series strives to help students develop a broader and deeper understanding of the nature of science by examining notable ideas and events in the history of science. Books in the series focus on the development and outcomes of atomic theory, cell theory, germ theory, evolution theory, plate tectonic theory, and more. All books clearly state the core idea and explore changes in thinking over time, methods of experimentation and observation, and societal impacts of these momentous theories and discoveries. Each volume includes a visual chronology; brief descriptions of important people; sidebars that highlight and further explain key events and concepts; "words in context" vocabulary; and, where possible, the words of the scientists themselves.

Through richly detailed examples from history and clear discussion of scientific ideas and methods, *The Importance of Scientific Theory* series furthers an appreciation for the essence of science and the men and women who devote their lives to it. As the authors of "Understanding the Scientific Enterprise: The Nature of Science in the Next Generation Science Standards" write, "With the addition of historical examples, the nature of scientific explanations assumes a human face and is recognized as an ever-changing enterprise."

IMPORTANT DATES IN THE HISTORY OF EVOLUTION THEORY

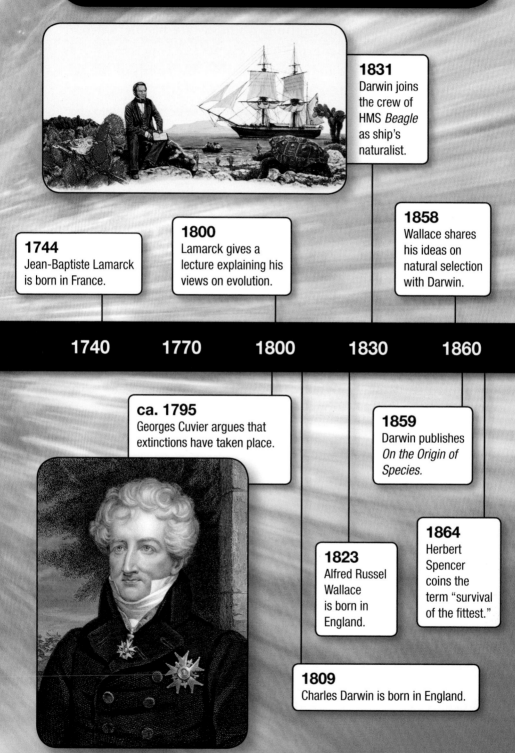

1831
Darwin joins the crew of HMS *Beagle* as ship's naturalist.

1858
Wallace shares his ideas on natural selection with Darwin.

1800
Lamarck gives a lecture explaining his views on evolution.

1744
Jean-Baptiste Lamarck is born in France.

1740	1770	1800	1830	1860

ca. 1795
Georges Cuvier argues that extinctions have taken place.

1859
Darwin publishes *On the Origin of Species.*

1864
Herbert Spencer coins the term "survival of the fittest."

1823
Alfred Russel Wallace is born in England.

1809
Charles Darwin is born in England.

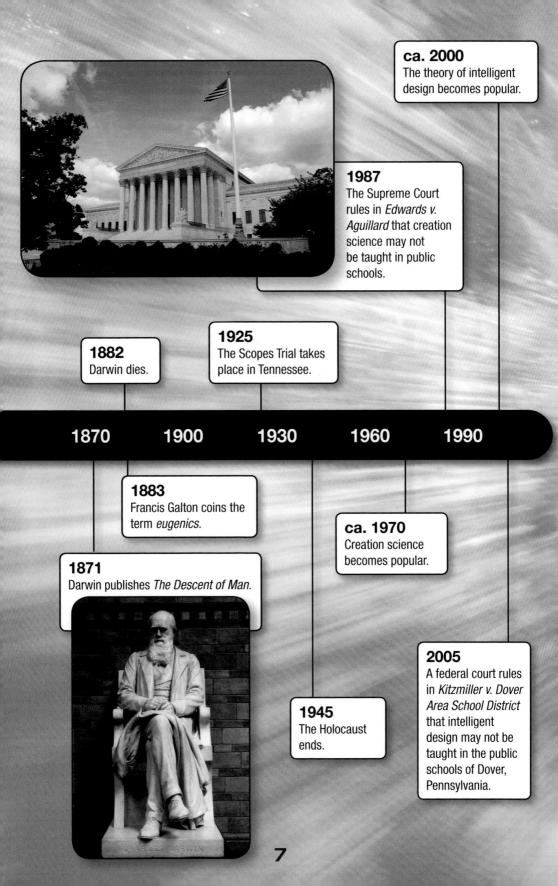

ca. 2000
The theory of intelligent design becomes popular.

1987
The Supreme Court rules in *Edwards v. Aguillard* that creation science may not be taught in public schools.

1925
The Scopes Trial takes place in Tennessee.

1882
Darwin dies.

1870   1900   1930   1960   1990

1883
Francis Galton coins the term *eugenics*.

ca. 1970
Creation science becomes popular.

1871
Darwin publishes *The Descent of Man*.

2005
A federal court rules in *Kitzmiller v. Dover Area School District* that intelligent design may not be taught in the public schools of Dover, Pennsylvania.

1945
The Holocaust ends.

INTRODUCTION

Evolution and Society

THE CORE IDEA

Over millions and millions of years, all living things on Earth have been changing in countless ways. In some cases the changes have been so great as to create an entirely new species, or group of similar organisms. The theory of evolution explains the mechanism for these changes. Evolution is based primarily on the idea of natural selection—that certain members of a species have and develop traits that are particularly useful for survival. Those individuals will have a greater chance of living long and living well, and will therefore have a good chance of passing their genes down to future generations. Variation in advantageous traits, in turn, can be explained partly by mutations, or random changes in the genes of living things. Mutations that prove useful to the organism are likely to become widespread in the population. Over time, through mutation and natural selection, entirely new species can emerge.

Of all the scientific principles and theories developed throughout history, few have been as controversial—or as influential—as the theory of evolution. Developed in the mid-1800s, primarily by British scientist Charles Darwin, the theory of evolution holds that the millions of animal and plant species that live on Earth are in a constant state of flux. Rather than existing in their present form throughout the history of the planet, they have changed continually over long periods of time in ways both great and small. For example, according to evolutionary theory, apes and humans share a common ancestor; today's birds are descended from dinosaurs; and the flowers, trees, and grasses of the modern world are related to one another in dozens of ways.

Evolutionary change is guided partly by mutations, or changes to the genetic material of living things. These mutations typically take place on an individual level, so any changed genes are present in only one member of the species at first. Most mutations damage the individual's chance of survival. A squirrel born with a gene that causes weakened leg muscles, for instance, will not manage to live for long. But a few mutations actually increase the chances that an individual will survive. If the individual reproduces, the mutations can be passed on to the individual's offspring and, over time, become common among the members of the species.

Whether a mutation takes hold in the general population is governed by a process called natural selection. The most advantageous mutations raise the odds that an individual will pass its genes down to the next generation. Salmon, for example, swim to find food, escape enemies, and reach the spawning grounds where they reproduce. A salmon with a mutation that allows it to swim farther and faster than ordinary salmon will increase its chances of surviving, reproducing, and passing on the new mutation. Biologists would say that the gene that creates better-swimming salmon is selected for within the population. Through natural selection more and more salmon will come to have this trait, as the salmon with the mutation reproduce and the ones without it struggle to survive.

Often, mutations result in only small modifications. When new mutations are introduced into a population of living things, individuals of that species may grow somewhat taller, develop slightly different coloration, or exhibit other minor changes—while clearly remaining members of the same species. In other cases, however, natural selection can lead to the formation of an entirely new species. That is particularly true when one group develops a mutation and another group does not. Two populations of once identical fish may diverge, for instance, with one developing a longer snout and sharper teeth while the other does not, or a type of bush common in two places may become much shorter in one spot while remaining unchanged in the other.

Evolution and Science

Scientists do not doubt that evolution is real. Evidence from genetics, anatomy, and other branches of science supports the notion

Sockeye salmon swim in the Adams River in British Columbia toward their spawning grounds. A salmon that swims farther and faster than other salmon would be more likely to survive, reproduce, and, most importantly, pass on these traits to their offspring .

that species have evolved in a myriad of ways over millions of years. "Nothing is static," writes scientist Norman D. Newell, discussing the natural world. "Yesterday things were different and the changes that we see taking place guarantee that tomorrow will not be like to-day."[1] Nonetheless, the reality of evolution has been frequently challenged since Darwin's time. Some of that debate has rested on religious grounds. Many Christian clerics of Darwin's era condemned the idea of evolution. As they saw it, Darwin was replacing God with an alarming emptiness. In Darwin's conception the world was governed not by a benevolent deity but by cold, indifferent chance.

This way of thinking remains common among conservative Christians today. Studies suggest that up to half of Americans have doubts about whether evolution is true. Their skepticism has frequently been an issue in politics, education, and other aspects of American civic life. On the one side are religious activists who argue that schools should teach alternatives to evolution in science class, since evolution, in their view, is "only a theory";[2] on the other are scientists who point to the enormous amount of evidence that evolution actually takes place. The debate is not helped by a frequent misunderstanding of how the word *theory* is used in science. Where *theory*, in ordinary speech, means simply *idea* or *assertion*, in science the word describes an explanation that fits all or nearly all of the available evidence. The phrase *theory of evolution*, then, does not mean that evolution is an educated guess, as many of its opponents believe; it means instead that evolution serves to explain scientific observations of the world.

The debate over the validity of evolution, then, has had an enormous effect on American society. But evolution has had an impact on thought and culture in other ways, too. In the early twentieth century, for example, some people extended evolutionary thinking into the social realm. As part of a movement often known as social Darwinism, they interpreted human behavior according to Darwin's ideas. Social Darwinists often attributed economic success and failure to evolutionary principles, for instance. Just as better-swimming salmon would eventually drive out the weaker swimmers, they argued, people well equipped for success would inevitably become rich and powerful. Social Darwinism played an important role in American social policies for many years.

> **WORDS IN CONTEXT**
>
> *natural selection*
>
> Process in which better-adapted organisms survive and reproduce.

And evolutionary theory remains significant today as well. The modern world is very different from the world of the past. Instant communication, ease of travel, and other factors have all brought the people of the globe closer together. Some theorists argue that this interconnectedness may bring an end to human evolution, since evolution most often occurs in isolated populations. Others, in contrast, argue that human evolution is still continuing—and may continue in ways that no one in previous generations could possibly have imagined, such as by controlling how genes are distributed in the human population. How these changes in evolution may affect humanity in the centuries to come is anyone's guess. But it is reasonable to assume that the topic of evolution will remain both important and controversial in the foreseeable future.

CHAPTER ONE

Before Darwin

Scientific thinking, as we understand the term today, got its start in Europe. But even in Europe, science in the years before 1800 was very much in its infancy. Many of the workings of the natural world remained a mystery to the scientific minds of the eighteenth century. Scientists of the period, for example, knew very little about germ theory—the idea that disease is frequently caused by microorganisms too small to be seen without magnification. Nor did they have any notion that Earth's outer shell consists of tectonic plates that drift from one place to another over billions of years, causing changes in the configurations of continents, islands, and oceans. Antibiotics were unknown, X-rays were unimaginable, and many of the chemical elements were as yet unidentified.

Moreover, much of what scientists of the 1600s and 1700s believed to be true was in fact completely erroneous. In the absence of germ theory, for example, most doctors and scientists of the period agreed that diseases were caused by an imbalance of "humors"— such as bile, phlegm, and blood—in the body. It was also widely believed that an invisible vapor, known as "bad air" or "miasma," could make people sick. Though today we know that fires need oxygen to burn, similarly, scientists through the late 1700s believed that fires were attributable to a material called phlogiston, which was supposedly released when objects were set aflame. And the idea of spontaneous generation, which held that inanimate objects such as iron, dust, and corpses could directly give rise to maggots, worms, and other forms of life, was accepted throughout Europe for many years.

Against this backdrop, it is no surprise that the possibility of evolution was little considered until the middle of the 1800s. In a world where scientific knowledge was rudimentary and often wrong, a complicated idea like evolution could not have gained much traction, even among the best educated and most thoughtful Europeans of the era. And indeed, the mere idea of evolution would have been laughable to the vast majority of Europeans until the beginning of the 1800s. For essentially all Europeans, evolution would not have helped in understanding or explaining the world. Nor did it fit the observations of the scientists who lived and worked throughout Europe during these years. It was not so much that evolution was carefully deliberated and then rejected; instead, it was unnecessary. As historian Carl Degler puts it, "Virtually none in early Christian Europe took seriously the idea that the present had emerged out of the past."[3] Until the mid-nineteenth-century research of Charles Darwin and other scientists, evolution was rarely if ever a part of the scientific discussion.

A Lack of Evidence

The great majority of Europeans before Darwin's time would have rejected the notion of evolution for two main reasons. The first was the lack of clear evidence of any change in any species of plant or animal. Certainly no such change had ever been observed by any specific person. Nor could it have been, since evolution typically takes place over centuries and millennia rather than during the lifetime of any individual human being. In theory, it might have been possible for a culture to witness and record small changes over an extended period of many human lifetimes, but the odds of that happening were small. If no one could see evolution taking place—and even the smartest, wisest Europeans of the era could not—there was no reason to believe it could happen.

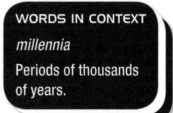

WORDS IN CONTEXT

millennia
Periods of thousands of years.

The scientific evidence for evolution, moreover, is largely contained in the fossil record—that is, in the bones, impressions of leaves, and other remains of plants and animals that indicate the breadth of changes in species over time. The bulk of this evidence, however, is buried well below the surface of Earth. Even by Darwin's time, European technologies were relatively simple. Other than mining and quarrying, few human activities brought people into contact with the world beneath their feet. A handful of geologists and other scientists

An alchemist, seated in his laboratory, searches for a way to change metal into gold. Because alchemists and other scientists of earlier eras had only rudimentary scientific knowledge, much of their work was based on flawed assumptions.

had gone digging in the riverbanks, quarries, and swamps of Europe, but these excavations focused primarily on the characteristics and arrangements of rocks, not specifically on bones or fossils. As a result, few Europeans before the 1800s ever saw a fossil or a bone of a species that no longer existed.

And if they did stumble upon a fossil that did not match the plants and animals they already knew, most people would have been unaware of the significance of what they had found. Even a scientist who discovered a completely unfamiliar fossil would have assumed that it was a remnant of a plant or animal from an existing species.

Perhaps the animal's descendants had abandoned Europe for Africa or Asia in the past; perhaps the plant was only to be found in dense European forests. One French writer of the early 1700s theorized that some fossilized plants "exist no more,"[4] but his was a minority opinion. Certainly the discovery of an unknown fossilized creature was not taken as proof that the organism's form had changed through natural processes over time.

Simply put, evolution made no practical sense. An individual horse, after all, was a horse; it had been a horse since its birth, and it would remain a horse until its death. The same, then, was undoubtedly true of species. Squirrels, spiders, and oak trees had been squirrels, spiders, and oak trees since the dawn of time, and their descendants would always be squirrels, spiders, and oak trees. To think otherwise would be to make a simple world much more complicated than it needed to be. In the absence of any evidence to the contrary, therefore, the people of Europe had no need to even consider the possibility that evolution might be real. As Degler describes it, evolution "was beyond their ken."[5]

WORDS IN CONTEXT

fossil

Remnant of an ancient animal or plant.

The Impact of Religion

In addition to the lack of evidence of evolutionary change, religious ideas also helped draw the Europeans of the period away from evolutionary thinking. Cultures across the world have their own creation stories, generally explaining how and why a creator being or beings made the universe, and Europeans of the 1700s were no exception. The vast majority of these Europeans were Christians, so the Bible was their primary source of religious information, and the Book of Genesis in the Old Testament provided the central account of how creation had taken place. In a time when the Bible was widely believed to be the unerring word of God, the Creation story was quite influential among Europeans in the years before Darwin.

However, the biblical Creation story left no room for evolution. According to Genesis, God did not populate the universe with microorganisms that gradually evolved into more complex forms of life.

On the contrary, Genesis reported that God spent six days creating the universe and filling the land, water, and sky with the same varieties of animals and plants that existed when the narrative was written. The account given in the first chapter of Genesis begins with the creation of light on the first day and the formation of the sky on the second. The third day includes not only the making of dry land and bodies of water, but the creation of plants. Next, on the fourth day, God placed the sun, moon, and stars in their orbits. The universe was rapidly taking shape.

All that remained, then, was the animal kingdom. As Genesis describes it, the fifth day was given over to the creation of birds and sea creatures. The sixth day, similarly, began with God making mammals, the so-called higher animals. Warm-blooded and designed to suckle their young, mammals were believed to be smarter than the birds and fish that were made before them; thus, they represented a step up in intelligence and awareness. Even so, these creatures were not the culmination of Creation. That was the making of human beings, which took place later on the sixth day. "Let us make mankind in our image, in our likeness" (Gen. 1:26), God commanded. By creating people as a reflection of himself, God left no doubt that humanity represented the pinnacle of what he had accomplished. "God saw all that he had made," the chapter concludes, "and it was very good. And there was evening, and there was morning—the sixth day" (Gen. 1:31).

Implications of Genesis

The account of Creation given in the first chapter of Genesis made excellent sense to the people of the ancient Middle East, the time and place that produced the narrative, and to the later Europeans who enthusiastically accepted it as a foundation of their own religious belief. Certainly the narrative was logical. The universe could not have had a sun and stars before there was any light, for example, and plants and animals could not have appeared until after Earth's surface had been divided into land and water. But the sequence also made sense for another reason. According to Genesis, God had given humankind dominion over the plants and animals. The people of Europe, like those of the early Middle East, were primarily farmers and herders. They

God creates the birds and sea creatures in this sixteenth-century painting by the Italian artist Jacopo Tintoretto. Adherence to the biblical Creation story made it difficult for people to accept the concept of evolution.

fed and cared for livestock and in turn used cattle and sheep for meat, milk, and other purposes; they sowed and nurtured crops and later turned the plants into food. As Genesis explains, they ruled over all the living things that surrounded them.

The Creation story in Genesis had important implications. One of these was the idea that humanity was special. Human beings, after all, had been made in God's own image. Alone among the animals— alone even among mammals—humans had the power of speech, the ability to reason, and an immortal soul. In addition, God had given over the rest of Creation to humans for their own use. In the words of Genesis, Earth was at the disposal of men and women "so that they may rule over the fish in the sea and the birds in the sky, over the livestock and all the wild animals, and over all the creatures that move along the ground" (Gen. 1:26). In the basic structure of bones and muscles, humans resembled other mammals and even some lower animals as well, but Genesis made it clear that in truth humanity had very little in common with these other creatures. Humans were unique.

Creation Stories and Evolution

Like the Creation story in the Bible, creation stories from other traditions generally assume that plants and animals have existed unchanged since the beginning of time. The creation story popular among the ancient Greeks, for example, differed from the biblical account mainly in that creation was the work of two gods rather than one. The story told how the god Prometheus made human beings in the image of the divine, while another god, Epimetheus, created the animals. The tale implies that both humans and other animals had remained in the same form since the moment of their creation.

The Mayan peoples of Central America likewise believed that life had been created by divine beings. In their account the gods had created the first people out of corn. According to the Mayans, the animals, too, were put on Earth in their current form; the story even emphasizes that the original animals could bark, howl, and make other typical animal sounds. And in one version of the creation story told among the aboriginal peoples of Australia, creation is the responsibility of the Sun Mother deity, who creates the plants simply by walking on Earth. Later in the narrative she creates fish, reptiles, and amphibians, followed by the higher animals.

The idea of a special creation orchestrated by one or more divine beings is in fact common in creation stories across the world. By leaving out any idea of evolution, the account given in the Book of Genesis is scarcely unusual.

A second important implication of Genesis was the idea of perfection. According to the Bible, God had created a flawless universe. The evil in the world, Genesis explained, came not from God's design but instead from other sources: Satan—the devil—on the one hand, the poor choices of humanity on the other. In the famous story of Adam and Eve, Genesis describes how the first couple, encouraged by a malevolent serpent, disobeyed God's order not to eat a piece of fruit in the Garden of Eden—and how the two of them were cast out of paradise forever as a result. The story reinforced the notion that even if people had fallen from God's grace, God's original creation had nevertheless been perfect.

That perfection, in turn, meant that God's work could not be improved upon. The natural world did not change and never would. The plants that Europeans grew and the animals they herded were exactly like the plants and animals God had made during the first days of Creation. Wheat plants could not suddenly start growing pine cones any more than pine trees would give grain; the teeth and hooves of sheep and cattle were distinct and always had been. It would have been blasphemous, then, to believe that since the Creation there had been any alterations, significant or otherwise, in the forms of these or any other living things. Though civilizations and cultures might come and go, the universe was essentially unchanging. As Ecclesiastes, another book of the Old Testament, puts it, "What God does lasts forever; to add to it or subtract from it is impossible" (Eccl. 3:14).

Contradictions and Inaccuracies

Despite the apparent assurance of the Bible, European scientists and philosophers of the early 1800s were noticing a growing number of potential contradictions between its words and the evidence of the natural world. At least one of these contradictions had been observed long before 1800. Whereas several biblical passages indicate that the sun revolves around Earth, the discoveries of Nicolaus Copernicus, Galileo Galilei, and other astronomers during the 1500s and 1600s proved that this was not the case. At first these scientists' claim that the sun was at the center of the solar system was hotly disputed. By 1800, though, their view was accepted by essentially all Europeans of science. To accept the evidence of astronomy, then, meant accepting that the Bible was not completely reliable as a source of information about the world.

As the 1800s began, more and more potential contradictions began to emerge. Genesis, for example, refers to Noah's Flood, a deluge that swamped the earth. But scientists became increasingly reluctant to accept this tale as the literal truth—partly because of practical questions such as where the water went when the flood receded, and partly because evidence from geology showed no indication of a single catastrophic flood. Nor did the timeline established by the Bible seem to fit the available evidence. The Old Testament includes genealogies that date back to Adam and Eve, implying that the earth is perhaps six thousand years old. "There was literally not time enough for [evolution],"[6] explains author Loren Eiseley. By the late 1700s, however, scientists were increasingly doubtful that a few thousand years was enough to account for all the changes in the geologic record. Scottish geologist James Hutton, for example, argued that Earth might actually be as much as a million years old.

And perhaps most damning of all, it was becoming abundantly clear that Earth had not, in fact, remained unchanged since its cre-

Augustine and Evolution

Although the theory of evolution was unknown in ancient times, several early thinkers did approach an evolutionary way of looking at the world. One of these was Augustine of Hippo (354–430), a North African bishop and theologian.

Augustine argued that each organism placed on Earth during the Creation had been endowed with the ability to change and grow. Over time, and under the right circumstances, these organisms might alter their shape and other important features to become something new. In Augustine's opinion, then, modern plants and animals could well have been descended from organisms that at the time of Creation had looked entirely different. Augustine reached this conclusion by analogy with seeds. The seed of a plant, after all, contains everything necessary to create that plant. Given sunlight, water, and soil, the seed will eventually develop into exactly the plant it was intended to become. In the same way, Augustine reasoned, the living things God placed on Earth during Creation carried the seeds of something more complex. As part of some divine plan, God would trigger the changes to turn the organisms into the familiar species of today.

Augustine's view, in the end, differed from evolution because he saw no role for random chance in the process. The changes organisms underwent, in his description, were the specific will of God. Still, the basic thrust of Augustine's outlook—that living things could change—did have much in common with Darwin's later argument.

French naturalist Georges Cuvier oversees preparations for a museum exhibit. From his work with prehistoric mammoth fossils and modern elephants, Cuvier concluded that extinctions could and did take place.

ation. Fossilized shells of a type found only in oceans, for example, could be found among the rocks on the faces of cliffs hundreds of feet above the sea. To forward-thinking scientists, this was a clear indication that these cliffs had been submerged at some point in the past. Rock layers in other places had been broken apart by underground forces; some had even been carried from one location to another. In the late 1700s French scientist Georges Cuvier showed that fossils of prehistoric mammoths differed from modern elephants "as much as, or more than, the dog differs from the jackal and the hyena";[7] since no one had ever seen a mammoth in the wild—and since such a large animal would be difficult to miss—he felt safe concluding that extinctions could and did take place.

The European scientists of the late 1700s and early 1800s were not, however, willing to reject the Bible entirely. On the contrary, they typically saw it as a source of great wisdom and as an invaluable spiritual guide, even if they preferred to view it more as metaphorically true than factual. Indeed, most scientists of the time did not believe that their work would take them farther away from God; rather, it would bring them closer to the divine. By studying the forces that acted to change Earth and the organisms that lived upon it, these thinkers argued, they would move ever nearer to understanding the mind of God. Nature, wrote British geologist Adam Sedgwick, was simply "the reflection of the power, wisdom, and goodness of God,"[8] and the study of nature was therefore the study of God himself. Though this perspective was not always widely shared, it was evidence of a shift in the thinking of many educated people of the time—a shift that would soon cause enormous repercussions in Europe and beyond.

CHAPTER TWO

A New Idea

The scientific discoveries of the late 1700s and early 1800s did not represent proof that evolution was real. On the contrary, most educated people of the time found it easy to explain the contradictions between Scripture and science without resorting to a new theory. The apparent age of Earth, for example, suggested to some that the biblical six days of creation were meant figuratively rather than literally—a change which certainly did not imply evolution. The fact that some living creatures had become extinct, similarly, could mean simply that God had tired of them, not that evolution was at work. And even though scientists now knew that Earth had undergone major physical changes throughout its history, that did not indicate that biological changes like evolution were also taking place.

But even if they did not directly accept the notion that a species could evolve, a growing number of scientists began wondering whether such a thing could happen. They increasingly recognized that many aspects of the natural world *had* changed, that the natural order was not *necessarily* perfect, and that the Bible was not perhaps *strictly* true. More and more, the thinking of scientists in the early 1800s reflected a new way of looking at the universe. Whether they were fully aware of it or not, a barrier had been crossed. The scholars of the era were beginning to approach science from an evolutionary perspective. The stage was set for a great new discovery.

Lamarck and Others

Born in 1809, Charles Darwin is justly given the most credit for developing the theory of evolution. But he was by no means alone. Even before Darwin's birth a number of earlier scholars had expressed ideas that in significant ways prefigured Darwin's. In 1794, for example, James Hutton argued that species best suited to their environments would be unlikely candidates for extinction, while "those which depart most from the best adapted constitution, will be the most liable to perish."[9] British physician William Charles Wells suggested as early as 1813 that variations in skin color might show that human beings had changed through time. And Darwin's grandfather, a naturalist named Erasmus Darwin, was drawn toward evolutionary thinking as well. Erasmus believed that all life on Earth had begun eons earlier as single-celled organisms. As Erasmus explained in verse, these organisms eventually became more complex, "Then as successive generations bloom, new powers acquire and larger limbs assume."[10]

The best known among these early evolutionists, however, was French scientist Jean-Baptiste Lamarck. Born in 1744, Lamarck proposed that every species contained a substance that he called nervous fluid. This fluid had the ability to transform each species over time, thus allowing it to take on a new form. As Lamarck saw it, these changes were purposeful, not random; they were designed to bring the species to a higher level of complexity—from a blade of grass to a tree, perhaps, or from a microorganism to a ladybug or mouse. The wide variety of life on Earth, Lamarck believed, was the result of this process.

Lamarck also believed that environmental factors often set the fluid into action. In one famous example, Lamarck suggested that giraffes originally had necks as short as those of any other animal their size. Because they were constantly stretching to reach the leaves of trees on the African savanna, though, more and more of this nervous fluid flowed into their necks. According to Lamarck, the fluid served to lengthen each individual giraffe's neck. When a long-necked giraffe reproduced, it passed this change on to its offspring. In this way, each generation of giraffes was born with an increasingly long neck, until finally the average giraffe was tall enough to munch the leaves from a comfortable standing position.

Rejection

The views of men like Wells and Lamarck were not well received by most scientists of the time. For some, even these small steps away from an ordered, planned universe smacked of atheism. As historian Carl Zimmer writes, Lamarck in particular appeared to be "reducing mankind and the rest of nature to the product of some unguided, earthly force."[11] For other observers, the problem was a lack of confirmation. If a nervous fluid actually existed in plants or animals, for example, no one could find any trace of it. Nor did the fossil record support Lamarck's contention that changes to species always made them more complex. According to the fossil record, plenty of extinct plants and animals were every bit as complex as modern living things. Finally, many scientists doubted that environmentally based changes in one animal could be passed down to the animal's offspring.

The French scientist Jean-Baptiste Lamarck suggested that the earliest giraffes had short necks. He believed that their constant stretching to reach the leaves of tall trees, over time and many generations, led to the lengthening of their necks.

Natural Selection and the Struggle for Life

In his work *On the Origin of Species*, Charles Darwin describes the process of natural selection in these words:

> We see beautiful adaptations everywhere in every part of the organic world. Again, it may be asked, how is it that varieties . . . become ultimately converted into good and distinct species, which in most cases obviously differ from each other far more than do the varieties of the same species? How do those groups of species . . . arise? All these results . . . follow inevitably from the struggle for life. Owing to this struggle for life, any variation, however slight and from whatever cause proceeding, if it be in any degree profitable to an individual of any species . . . will tend to the preservation of that individual, and will generally be inherited by its offspring. The offspring, also, will thus have a better chance of surviving, for, of the many individuals of any species which are periodically born, [only] a small number can survive. I have called this principle, by which each slight variation, if useful, is preserved, by the term of Natural Selection.

Charles Darwin, *On the Origin of Species*. New York: Collier, 1909, p. 77.

In England in particular, the views of these thinkers were enthusiastically rejected by the most influential scientists of the time. Erasmus Darwin, for example, who was never a member of Britain's inner circle of scientists, was perceived largely as a crank and an embarrassment; his willingness to break social norms by having out-of-wedlock children after the death of his wife did nothing to support his cause. And openly admiring the works of Lamarck was a good way to be shunned by the most powerful scholars in the nation. When Adam Sedgwick found several fossils that suggested an organism had changed form over a period of many years, he reported his results with great circumspection. "I do not mean by this to vindicate [confirm] the transmutation [change] of species," Sedgwick wrote. "I only wish to state a fact of general observation."[12]

Indeed, the orthodox way of thinking about the universe in Britain in the early 1800s still focused on the world as God's creation. The intricate workings of the universe, the regular changing of the seasons, the adaptations of animals and plants to their environments—all indicated the hand of a deity at work in creating and planning the world. In an influential text published in 1802, scholar William Paley likened the universe to a watch. Anyone coming upon a watch in a field, Paley noted, would assume that the watch had been constructed by a person: It was too useful and too complex to have been made by random events. In the same way, Paley reasoned, the world could not have been created by chance. "Design must have had a designer," he wrote. "That designer must have been a person. That person is GOD."[13]

Nonetheless, the debate over whether some form of evolution had taken place was far from settled, even in Britain. And although the forces of scientific orthodoxy continued to hold the upper hand through the first decades of the 1800s, their position was not as powerful as they believed. Each new scientific discovery, it seemed, cast further doubt on the hypothesis that Earth's various plants and animals had always existed in their present forms. Little by little, opposition to standard Bible-based explanations was rising. Although there was still no clear evidence of evolution, and although no one yet understood how new traits might be passed on to future generations, younger scholars increasingly found themselves wondering whether evolutionary ideas might in fact be accurate.

> **WORDS IN CONTEXT**
>
> *hypothesis*
> Suggested explanation for observations in science.

Darwin

Charles Darwin was one of these young scholars, though he came to this position with some reluctance. Unlike his grandfather, Charles was neither a free spirit nor a rebel. Nonetheless, Darwin's education had included exposure to some evolutionary ideas. While studying in Scotland, for example, Darwin had become acquainted with a zoologist named Robert Grant. Unusual among British scientists of the day, Grant found Lamarck's ideas not only intriguing but quite possibly true, and Grant was happy to share his interpretations of Lamarckian thought with Darwin. Most historians doubt that Darwin found Grant's ideas compelling, but it seems likely that much of what Grant had to say did make some impression upon the young student. As one of Darwin's biographers puts it, Darwin's studies in Scotland ultimately guided him to see evolution as "a living and potentially credible doctrine."[14]

In 1831, barely into his twenties, Darwin accepted a position as a naturalist on the ship HMS *Beagle*. The *Beagle* had been assigned to undertake a multiyear voyage mapping the coasts of South America, and Darwin's work was to collect and write about specimens of the various plants and animals of the region. Though Darwin turned out to be prone to seasickness, he found the journey deeply fascinating, and he relished his time studying ferns, finches, and other living

While traveling through the Galapagos Islands, naturalist Charles Darwin discovered that nearly every island had its own distinctive species of finch. The shapes and sizes of their beaks, as seen in his drawings (pictured), illustrate some of the differences between these species.

1. Geospiza magnirostris.
3. Geospiza parvula.
2. Geospiza fortis.
4. Certhidea olivasca.

things as the *Beagle* slowly made its way along the South American shoreline. When the ship returned to Britain in 1836, Darwin had a treasure trove of specimens, observations, and data.

Most of all, though, he had questions. As Darwin sorted through the information he had gathered in his five years abroad, he was struck by the remarkable variations in species he had encountered. He was especially intrigued by some of the species he had found on islands and island groups, such as the Galapagos chain in the Pacific Ocean west of Ecuador. In particular, when he and other scientists examined the data they realized that nearly every island in the Galapagos chain had its own distinctive species of finch—a small songbird common throughout much of the world. The finches were easy to tell apart by the shapes and sizes of their beaks; as Darwin wrote, they were as a group "slightly differing in structure."[15] According to the standard scientific thinking of the day, the finches had been made that way by God. But Darwin was not satisfied with this answer. Why, he wondered, should there be a different type of finch for every island, when the great mass of finches on the South American mainland showed little or no variation?

As Darwin worked on the problem, he began to wonder if the reason might involve evolution. Perhaps, he speculated, there had originally been a single species of finch in the Galapagos. Over time, the finches could have settled on various islands. On some of these islands, Darwin hypothesized, the finches had developed beaks well suited to cracking and eating seeds; presumably those were islands where seeds were plentiful and bugs, another common food source for finches, were not. On other islands, where the reverse was true, the finches had developed beaks better designed for grabbing and eating insects. According to this explanation, the finches had diverged from one another because of the needs and demands of their environments. The hypothesis fit the facts.

Natural Selection

Darwin's conclusion was more or less consistent with the thinking of Lamarck and other scientists. Given the reluctance of British scholars to accept Lamarckian ideas, however, Darwin chose at first to keep his evolutionary thoughts to himself. He had another reason for silence, too. Darwin was deeply unconvinced by Lamarck's belief that the environment could cause major changes to individual animals and plants, changes that could then be passed on to the next generation. In his estimation, there was no evidence whatsoever for this hypothesis. As a result, until he could come up with a plausible mechanism by which plants and animals transmitted changes to their descendants, Darwin was unwilling to publish his ideas.

Over the next few years Darwin devoted most of his time to the question of how such changes might be passed down. He studied subjects from dog breeding to agriculture; he read the works of biologists, social reformers, and others. At last, in 1844 he found an answer. Lamarck, Darwin concluded, had it backward. An animal or plant did not change to meet the demands of its environment. On the contrary, the demands of the environment favored those animals and plants that were best equipped to survive—and thrive—in that setting. "If a population of birds ended up on a Galapagos island," Zimmer explains, "the individual birds that were best suited to life on [that] island would produce the next generation. And with enough time, these changes could produce a new species of bird."[16]

Darwin had discovered what is now referred to as natural selection. In concept, natural selection is simple enough. It is based in part on the science of genetics, or the way in which characteristics are passed from one organism to its descendants. Each living thing, however small, contains genes—strings of matter that help determine the characteristics of that particular organism. Though genetics was not well understood in Darwin's time, it was nevertheless known in outline.

WORDS IN CONTEXT

genetics

The study of how traits are inherited.

People such as farmers, dog breeders, and pigeon fanciers all relied on genetics to carry out their work. To produce a strong, patient dog for herding sheep, for example, a dog owner would likely breed two adult dogs that already exhibited these characteristics. Not all offspring of this pair would have the desired traits, but many would. Similarly, to increase crop yields, a farmer might cross two grain plants that were especially hardy.

Charles Darwin, pictured in an 1883 portrait, discovered the scientific concept of natural selection. Fully expecting a negative backlash, he waited more than a decade to reveal his carefully and thoroughly researched findings.

In addition, natural selection relies on the fact that no two individuals of a given species are precisely identical. Just as any two human beings are different, so too are two individual cows, two individual ferns, or two individual butterflies. These individuals, then, will be slightly differently suited to their environment. If two giraffes live on an African plain where the best leaves grow high above the ground, then—all other things being equal—the giraffe that happens to be taller will get more to eat. This giraffe has a better chance of living longer and will be more likely to produce offspring. Its genes—including the gene that governs height—will continue into the next generation. Over time the genes of the less-favored shorter giraffe may be eliminated from the population altogether. The key, however, is the phrase *over time*. "We see nothing of these slow changes in progress," Darwin explained, "until the hand of time has marked the long lapses of ages."[17]

Genes and Mutations

Darwin's view included one other important idea. Though in most cases genes remain unchanged when they are passed from one generation to the next, it is also possible for genes to be altered during this process. This is known as genetic mutation. Many mutations are negative; they make it more difficult for a plant or animal to survive, and so they do not generally become a part of the gene pool. Others are neutral; they do not affect the ability of the organism to survive or reproduce, and they may or may not become a part of the genetic material of the species. But a few mutations are positive. They have the effect of giving the individual an edge over others of its species and may be carried down into future generations. According to Darwin's hypothesis, these mutations can not only change the gene pool of a species, but might also lead to the establishment of a completely new species. "Species have been modified," Darwin wrote, "chiefly through the natural selection of numerous successive, slight, favorable variations."[18]

Despite his careful research and thorough understanding of his subject, Darwin continued to keep his arguments private for well over a decade. Even then he might not have gone public with his findings if he had not learned that another British scientist, Alfred Russel Wallace, was independently developing some remarkably similar ideas. Spurred into action, Darwin hurried to complete his work. In 1859 Darwin published his influential—and massive—book *On the*

Alfred Russel Wallace

Other than Darwin himself, no historical figure is more closely associated with the theory of evolution than Alfred Russel Wallace. Fourteen years younger than Darwin, Wallace had a deep interest in zoology and was an enthusiastic explorer and social reformer as well. Known throughout his career for advocating unpopular scientific ideas, Wallace was an early adopter of Lamarck's notion that animals could and did undergo changes.

Before long, however, Wallace became unhappy with Lamarck's hypothesis that nervous fluid caused animals to undergo physical changes that could be passed down to their offspring. Casting around for another possible mechanism for evolutionary change, he hit upon natural selection sometime in the mid-1850s. "It occurred to me to ask the question, why do some die and some live?" he recalled afterward. "And the answer was clearly, on the whole the best fitted live."

Wallace and Darwin knew each other before Wallace had considered the possibility of natural selection and had shared some ideas in a series of letters. Together, Darwin and Wallace presented a paper on evolution, and Wallace published an essay on his ideas shortly before *On the Origin of Species* appeared. However, Wallace never got full credit for his work on evolution. Darwin was older and better known, and he had a good deal more social standing than the less high-born Wallace. In any case, Wallace seemed content to be given some credit for what he had accomplished, and he became one of Darwin's most enthusiastic supporters after *On the Origin of Species* was published.

Quoted in Andrew Berry, ed., *Infinite Tropics: An Alfred Russel Wallace Anthology*. New York: Verso, 2002, p. 51.

Origin of Species. The book summed up most—but not all—of Darwin's thinking at the time. Even so, Darwin was far from convinced that the book would be well received. "God knows what the public will think,"[19] he sighed upon the book's publication. As it turned out, he was right to be concerned.

CHAPTER THREE

Backlash

Many scientists, both in Britain and beyond, were deeply impressed by Darwin's work. Alfred Russel Wallace, of course, embraced Darwin's theories. British botanist Joseph Hooker became a staunch ally. So did a young British zoologist named Thomas Huxley, who had come to evolution through something of an evolutionary process himself. Originally scornful of the notion that living species could ever change, Huxley had become a convert after a long discussion with Darwin a few years before the publication of *On the Origin of Species*. Other scientists championed Darwin's ideas, too. But these scholars knew that Darwin's theories would be controversial. Huxley, for one, anticipated a bitter war of words ahead. "I am sharpening up my claws and beak in readiness,"[20] he told Darwin.

Indeed, negative reaction was swift and sometimes vitriolic. In some ways the opposition was perhaps predictable. Many important scientific theories have met with widespread opposition. Church officials forced Galileo to recant his position that Earth revolves around the sun. Geologist Alfred Wegener, who argued that continents drifted very slowly from one part of Earth to another, was mocked by many of his scientific colleagues. "If we are to believe in Wegener's hypothesis," a fellow geologist complained, "we must forget everything which has been learned in the past 70 years and start all over again."[21] To expect instant approval of a theory that shook the foundations of science as much as evolution did, then, would be unrealistic.

Still, the debate over evolution has lasted much longer than the debates over most other scientific theories. Wegener, for example, proposed his theory in about 1912, and in less than seventy-five years his ideas had become accepted by virtually everyone. But evolution was different. Seventy-five years after the publication of *On the Ori-*

gin of Species the argument about evolution was, if anything, continuing to ramp up. More than a century and a half after Darwin's ideas became widely known, millions of Americans continue to reject the notion that evolution is true. Nor does it seem likely that the evolution debate will be settled anytime in the near future. Few scientific questions, then, have been as long-lasting—or as divisive—as the debate over evolution.

Science and Religion

The initial wave of resistance to Darwinian ideas rested partly on scientific grounds. Some critics were concerned that Darwin had misinterpreted evidence, drawn unwarranted conclusions, or ignored proper scientific protocols. Several scholars argued, for example, that evolutionary changes caused by natural selection would have required many more years than Earth had existed—a misconception stemming from severe underestimates of the age of the universe. Others pointed out that Darwin's theory lacked an explanation of how life had originally formed on Earth. And still others argued that genetic mutations were extremely unlikely to persist within a population of plants or animals. No matter how beneficial the mutation might be to an individual member of a species, these people contended, the odds were that it would quickly be bred out of the population.

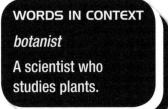

WORDS IN CONTEXT

botanist

A scientist who studies plants.

Though these objections sharply challenged Darwin's ideas, they were posed by scientists. Darwin and his followers could talk to them using a common vocabulary and a shared set of understandings about the way the world worked. These scientists could be brought to an evolutionary way of thinking with more science and better science—and in fact, that is exactly what happened. New experiments carried out in the 1860s and 1870s convinced many doubters that Darwin's theory made sense. Earlier misconceptions, such as underestimates of the real age of the universe, were gradually corrected. And of course some scientists merely needed time to process Darwin's revolutionary ideas. In any case, by the 1880s scientific opinion was squarely on the side of evolutionary theory; and since

1900 nearly all serious scientists have accepted the theory of evolution in outline, even if they have quibbled with some of the details.

That eventual acceptance of evolution did not apply to everyone, however. From the initial publication of Darwin's theories down to the present day, the idea of evolution has been repeatedly challenged by those who see it as incompatible with Christian teachings about God, the Bible, and the special place in the natural world occupied by humankind. Led in England, America, and elsewhere by ministers and their political allies, these critics have found Darwin's ideas unacceptable, even repugnant. Over the years, most criticisms of the theory of evolution have come from this quarter.

The Descent of Man

Darwin expected that challenges would come from religious leaders. He knew that some would balk at any notion that species could ever change. But he also knew that the most contentious part of his theory, at least for religious leaders, would involve the application of evolutionary thought to human beings. Though Darwin said very little about human evolution in *On the Origin of Species*, it was clear to any reader of the book that the evolutionary changes Darwin described applied to people, too. And in 1871, when Darwin published a new book called *The Descent of Man*, he made these connections explicit. Scientifically speaking, there was no reason to exempt humanity from the forces that created cats and catfish, daffodils and dragonflies. Evolution applied to all life—including humans.

To many religious leaders Darwin's work was indeed unacceptable—in particular because it eliminated humanity's special status. Adam Sedgwick, who in addition to being a geologist was also an ordained minister, spoke for many religious leaders when he complained about evolutionary theory. "I have read your book with more pain than pleasure," he told Darwin in a letter. If people came to believe that random chance, not divine guidance, governed the universe, he added, "humanity . . . would suffer a damage that might brutalise it, and sink the human race."[22] When Darwin's supporters recommended that he receive a national honor for his work, religious advisers to Britain's queen Victoria vetoed the idea. By replacing God's will, design, and loving care with a theory that emphasized natural

A color-enhanced 1871 caricature of Charles Darwin as half man-half ape illustrates contemporary hostility toward his book The Descent of Man. *Darwin clearly stated in this book that evolution applied to all living things, including human beings.*

forces, they warned Victoria, Darwin was moving toward atheism and blasphemy.

Many religious leaders believed, too, that acceptance of evolution would have grim consequences for society. In their eyes religion played

Darwin and Richard Owen

Charles Darwin was prepared to be attacked by fellow scientists. Still, he did not expect the degree of hostility he received from a British scholar named Richard Owen. Owen was well acquainted with Darwin—he had helped Darwin identify some of his specimens from the voyage of the *Beagle*—and he was by all accounts a brilliant man. But Owen was by no means ready to accept evolutionary theory, and he seemed to take Darwin's ideas as a personal affront.

Soon after *On the Origin of Species* was published, an unsigned review of it appeared in a Scottish periodical. It soon became clear that the author of the review was none other than Owen. His opinion of the book was extremely low, and he made no attempt to sugarcoat his words. *On the Origin of Species*, Owen wrote at one point, was "an abuse of science."

Darwin was deeply wounded by the intensity of this attack. Of all the negative reviews he received—and there were many—this was probably the one that hurt him the most. "It is painful to be hated in the intense degree with which Owen hates me," he commented. But Darwin, of course, did not recant his theory to please Owen, and Owen went to his grave insistent that Darwin was completely and utterly misguided. Not surprisingly, the two men never reconciled.

Quoted in Carl Zimmer, *Evolution: The Triumph of an Idea.* New York: HarperCollins, 2001, p. 51.

an essential role in establishing important values for human behavior. The Old Testament, for example, lists the Ten Commandments, rules of conduct dictated directly by God to humanity. Without God at the center of the universe, these clerics worried, there would be no moral authority to the Bible—and consequently no moral authority to these or any similar rules. "If we were nothing but a variation on an ape," Zimmer sums up, "then what became of morality?"[23] In a world governed by chance rather than by design, it seemed that nothing would prevent people from acting just as they pleased. Society, in short, was hanging by a very slender thread.

Darwin, Religion, and Politics

Not all Christian leaders of Darwin's time were opposed to evolutionary theory. On the contrary, many of the more progressive ministers and theologians of the era were drawn to Darwin's ideas. Some of these leaders were already inclined to see the Bible less as a history of actual events and more as a metaphor; for them, it was easy to accept that the Creation story in Genesis was metaphorical as well. Others were convinced by the growing weight of scientific evidence supporting Darwin's theory. As time passed, moreover, older ministers and bishops, those inclined to judge the theory more harshly, began to retire or die; the younger clerics who took their places were less willing to reject Darwinism out of hand.

Still, objections to evolution on religious grounds continued. Before long these objections spread into the political realm—particularly in the United States. In 1904, for example, American presidential candidate William Jennings Bryan spoke out against Darwinism in terms echoing those used by Sedgwick several decades earlier. "I object to the Darwinian theory," said Bryan, "because I fear we shall lose the consciousness of God's presence in our daily life, if we must accept the theory that through all the ages no spiritual force has touched the life of man."[24] Bryan was not a Biblical literalist—he was willing to acknowledge that Creation might have taken longer than six days—but he was not willing to concede that evolution was real, and he was particularly unwilling to accept that it had anything to do with human beings.

Before long, fearing the supposedly immoral influence of evolution, political and religious leaders in several states began working to pass laws that would ban the teaching of evolution in public schools. In 1925 Tennessee approved a bill that forbade instructors from teaching "any theory that denies the story of the Divine Creation of man as taught in the Bible, and [arguing] instead that man had descended from a lower order of animal."[25] Believing that the law violated the United States Constitution, the American Civil Liberties Union (ACLU)—an organization dedicated to ensuring that government does not trample the rights of its citizens—decided to pay the legal fees and possible penalties for any Tennessee teacher willing to challenge the law. John Scopes, who worked at a school in the small town of Dayton, agreed to do so. Scopes told authorities that he had taught evolution in his classroom. He was arrested and fined, and the case eventually went to trial.

The Scopes Trial

The trial became one of the major events of the decade. Newspapers from across the country sent reporters; radio stations broadcast updates directly from Dayton. There were two main reasons for the excitement. One involved changing views about the country. The twenties were a time when many believed that America was rapidly breaking into two separate and very different parts: one increasingly secular, urban, and forward looking; the other old-fashioned, rural, and focused on Christianity. The battle over evolution pitted ordinary Protestants hoping to keep God in a place of primacy against modern scholars and scientists looking to change the traditional values that had prevailed for hundreds of years. The clash between the two ways of thinking was compelling.

The interest in the trial also had to do with star power. As the trial date approached, both the ACLU and the prosecution announced that they would be using well-known attorneys to argue the case. Civil libertarian Clarence Darrow, noted for his intelligence and caustic wit, represented Scopes; Bryan, also a famous orator, led the prosecution. Rather than arguing about whether Scopes had broken the law or whether the law was constitutional, Darrow and Bryan turned the trial into a debate over evolution. Bryan lamented that children were being taught that humans were simply one species among thousands of mammals. Darrow, in turn, put Bryan on the witness stand and barraged him with questions designed to showcase inconsistencies in the Bible. Bryan was forced to admit that much of the Bible seemed beyond his understanding. "I believe in creation," he announced at one point, "and if I am not able to explain it I will accept it."[26]

Many of Bryan's supporters were pleased with how he had handled himself in the exchanges with Darrow. The proponents of evolution, however, believed they had scored a great victory, and Darrow

> **WORDS IN CONTEXT**
>
> *constitutional*
> According to the Constitution.

Renowned attorney Clarence Darrow (standing in foreground) listens to the 1925 Scopes Trial proceedings. Darrow represented biology teacher John Scopes, who was prosecuted for teaching evolution in his Tennessee classroom.

was convinced that he had emerged triumphant. "I made up my mind to show the country what an ignoramus he was," Darrow crowed, referring to Bryan, "and I succeeded."[27] In the end, the jury ruled against Scopes. He was found guilty of breaking the law and fined $100, though the conviction and fine were later overturned on a technicality. Few on Scopes's side were particularly upset, however. As evolution supporters saw it, Darrow's questioning of Bryan had embarrassed the antievolution movement. And indeed, organized opposition to evolution did appear to dwindle over the next few decades.

Creation Science and Intelligent Design

Any drop in antievolution sentiment, however, was temporary. In the 1960s and 1970s a new political movement known as creation science began taking shape. This movement was similar in many ways to the antievolution movement led by Bryan several decades before. Its adherents, nearly all of them Christians, accepted the biblical account of Creation as the literal truth. In this view, Earth was only a few thousand years old, a cataclysmic worldwide flood had taken place soon after the earth's creation, and evolution was a myth. What separated creation science from earlier objections to Darwin, though, was the embrace of the term *science* to describe what the movement believed. Indeed, those active in the movement often inverted traditional lan-

A panel from a 2014 exhibit at the Creation and Earth History Museum in Santee, California, presents the creationist point of view about evolution. That view characterizes evolution as a religious belief unsupported by scientific evidence.

THE EVOLUTION ILLUSION

The evolution of man from an ape-like primate is nothing more than an illusion created from man's imagination.

Try to touch the ape and "cave man" to see another illusion.

guage by referring to evolution as a religious belief unsupported by scientific evidence. "It is not science," argued Ken Ham, a leader of the antievolution forces; "it is a belief system about the past."[28]

The emphasis on the scientific part of creation science was not an accident. By calling the doctrine a form of science, backers of the idea hoped to suggest that creation science was every bit as respectable—and as academic a discipline—as any other area of scientific knowledge. The movement, however, was not particularly successful. Though supporters of creation science did a reasonably good job of getting publicity for their movement, they were less effective in bringing about change. In part, this was because those who accepted creation science tended to link their arguments to their Christian religious beliefs. Since the US Constitution bars government from favoring one religious belief over another, courts usually proved unwilling to allow creation science to be taught in schools. A Supreme Court ruling in 1987 gave this perspective the force of law, forbidding American public schools from teaching creation science at all.

More recently, opponents of evolution have tried a somewhat different tack: intelligent design. In many ways intelligent design is similar to creation science, but the two are not identical. Like creation science, for example, intelligent design rejects natural selection and assumes that life was created as a deliberate act by a designer; but most advocates of intelligent design do not publicly identify this designer as the Christian God. In this way they avoid the constitutional question of religion that presented

> **WORDS IN CONTEXT**
>
> *intelligent design*
>
> The idea that life was deliberately formed by an aware being.

an obstacle for adherents of creation science. Partly as a result, intelligent design has made inroads into education in a way that creation science never did. In places such as the state of Kansas and the town of Dover, Pennsylvania, school officials incorporated the principles of intelligent design into the curriculum. Their argument has been that evolution is a theory, not a fact, so alternative interpretations should be studied in science classes as well.

Many of these attempts have not been completely successful, however. In Kansas, several state board of education members who supported intelligent design were voted out of office the following year, and the new board members quickly rescinded the decision to teach intelligent design in state schools. In Pennsylvania, a judge ruled that since intelligent design was not truly scientific, the Dover schools could not teach it as science—and as in Kansas, school board members who had voted for intelligent design lost their seats. None-

"Breathtaking Inanity"

In October 2004 the school board in Dover, Pennsylvania, adopted a resolution requiring science teachers to read their biology students a statement on evolution. The statement identified evolution as nothing but a theory, and it urged students to seek out other possible explanations for the abundance and variety of species on Earth. As it happened, the statement provided one specific suggestion of an alternative hypothesis: intelligent design. When science teachers in the district refused to read the statement, the task was carried out by administrators instead.

While some Dover residents were pleased with the resolution, many others were not, and several filed suit. They claimed that the purpose of the statement was to inject religion into the classroom, and they asserted further that intelligent design was not in fact scientific. In December 2005 Judge John Jones agreed with them. In his decision he accused the board of "thrust[ing] an untestable alternative hypothesis grounded in religion into the science classroom," and he drew a sharp distinction between the "good science" of evolutionary theory and the unscientific claims of intelligent design. Leaving no doubt about where he stood on the matter, Jones also dismissed the board's original decision as an example of "breathtaking inanity."

Though Jones's decision applied solely to Dover, many people believe that other school boards decided not to try passing antievolution measures of their own for fear that Jones's ruling would eventually be used against them as well.

Quoted in Sean Scully, "'Breathtaking Inanity': How Intelligent Design Flunked Its Test Case," *Time*, December 20, 2005.

theless, the movement continues to fight for inclusion of intelligent design principles in American schools. In this way it is carrying on a long tradition of opposition to the theory of evolution—opposition that stretches back more than a century and a half, all the way to the initial publication of *On the Origin of Species*. What will happen on this front in the next few years and decades is anyone's guess, but it is certainly unlikely that the debate over evolution in schools will end anytime soon.

CHAPTER FOUR

Social Darwinism

Fearing criticism from religious leaders and others, Charles Darwin was initially reluctant to publicize his view that evolutionary theory applied to humans as well as to other living things. His fears were justified, as many people vehemently attacked him and his supporters for suggesting that humans might not have been created in God's image. The notion that humanity was merely another version of monkeys or apes, made different from these close relatives only by random chance rather than through divine design, was deeply disturbing for many, and Darwin and his followers were roundly condemned for their views.

In another way, however, Darwin need not have worried. During the late 1800s and early 1900s many influential thinkers not only accepted that Darwin's evolutionary ideas applied to people but eagerly extended his theories to explain the workings of society as well. Often known as social Darwinists, these people reasoned that the ultimate effect of evolution was to divide species into winners and losers. The winners, of course, were those that not only survived but thrived. They were the best at finding food, they expanded over wide swaths of territory, and they increased steadily in numbers. The losers were weaker and slower, less able to obtain and process food. They were outcompeted at every step, and their populations shrank as they received less and less of what was necessary for survival.

If this is the way of nature, social Darwinists reasoned, it might also be the way of human society. In this view individual people—and sometimes whole ethnic or racial groups—could be classed as winners and losers, just as evolutionary theory did with species. As social Darwinists saw it, some people were simply better equipped than others for survival in a competitive world. They were smarter and healthier, more creative and ambitious, and physically and emotionally stronger to boot. Just as successful species dominated the natural world, it was the destiny of better-equipped human beings to amass wealth and power and to become the leaders of society. Social Darwinism was quite popular among political and economic thinkers of the late 1800s and early 1900s. It was influential in setting social policy in the United States and elsewhere.

"Survival of the Fittest"

As with most important ideas, Darwin's theory of evolution was complex. Many people found it easy, however, to distill Darwin's thinking down to a few basic principles. One of the most obvious of these principles was competition, which was certainly an essential part of natural selection. Darwin described a world in which living things were engaged in a perpetual struggle with members of other species—and very often with other members of their own. Trees were engaged in a competition to see which could get more sunlight. Prey animals were engaged in a competition to conceal themselves most effectively from predators, who in turn competed to catch the choicest prey animals. Sometimes one species might have the upper hand, sometimes another, but competition was constant.

Though Darwin was well aware of the competitive aspects of nature, his works did not directly expand the notion of competition into the realm of human behavior. Others, however, were quick to make that connection. Among the first was British philosopher and scientist Herbert Spencer, who read *On the Origin of Species* soon after it appeared in 1859 and found it deeply intriguing. Several years later, Spencer published a book in which he used the phrase "survival of the fittest"[29] to describe the competitive aspects of natural selection. The "fittest," as he used the term, included those species best suited to their environments and to the conditions of the world, the ones most likely to flourish and to reproduce. Evolutionary theory, Spencer argued, was essentially a contest in which those best prepared for the rigors of the natural world survived and reproduced, and those less well prepared did neither.

A salmon succumbs to the powerful bite of a coastal brown bear in Alaska. In his theory of evolution, Darwin described a world in which living things perpetually compete to survive. Over time, this idea was distorted and applied to economics, intelligence, race, and more.

At the same time, Spencer took the notion of competition beyond the realm of nature. Deeply interested in the social sciences, Spencer saw parallels between evolutionary thinking and some of the economic ideas he had been grappling with before reading Darwin's book. In his formulation, just as plants and animals competed with one another for scarce resources—territory, sunlight, food—so too did people compete with one another for economic resources, such as land, money, and goods. The people who were most likely to succeed in life, as Spencer viewed it, were those who had certain inborn advantages, notably intelligence, health, thrift, persistence, and ambition.

The Rich and the Poor

Darwin liked the phrase "survival of the fittest." He used it, giving full credit to Spencer, in later editions of *On the Origin of Species*.

Others liked the phrase, too, and in the popular imagination "survival of the fittest" soon became almost synonymous with evolutionary theory. Many thinkers, moreover, agreed with Spencer that evolutionary ideas not only could but should be applied to human behavior, and that evolution had a great deal to say about why the world was so obviously unequal. Clearly, they concluded, the people with the most wealth had characteristics, whether obvious or hidden, that inevitably led them to success. Thus, these observers argued, the wealthy had gotten their riches by virtue of being better than everyone else. As society's best, they deserved the success they had achieved.

In addition to clarifying why the rich and powerful had so much, social Darwinism also provided a convenient explanation for why the poor had so little. Reasoning again from Darwin's argument that less successful species in the wild were simply less well equipped to survive, social Darwinists assumed that the poor were poor because they lacked the qualities that drove the well-off and powerful to achieve. It was a short step from there to the conclusion that poverty was inevitable. Just as there were winners and losers in the fields and forests of the natural world, there were winners and losers among human beings. As one historian writes, to the social Darwinists "biology was destiny."[30]

Social Darwinists did not necessarily blame the poor for their condition. Many were sympathetic to the plight of the impoverished. But virtually all social Darwinists assumed that the poorest members of society were poor for the simple reason that they were lacking in intelligence, drive, or some other important quality shared by the more successful. It was unfortunate; it was sad; it was unfair; but it was, social Darwinists agreed, the way of the world. The poor, in this view, were losers in the game of natural selection. They were being outperformed by the better-equipped rich in society, just as certain species in the natural world were pushed out of the best territories and denied the best food by competitors of their own. These species could not be expected to overcome their many disadvantages and suddenly become winners in the struggle for resources—and neither could the poor.

Economics and Race

Particularly in the United States the message of social Darwinism quickly entered the political realm. The American economy of the late 1800s and early 1900s was largely based

on laissez-faire capitalism—the idea that people should be allowed to make as much money as they could without interference from government. Business leaders like Andrew Carnegie and John D. Rockefeller made enormous sums of money during this period, benefiting greatly from a lack of government regulation or oversight. "There is nothing detrimental to human society" about the wealthy becoming even wealthier, Carnegie argued, "and much that is . . . beneficial."[31] James J. Hill, a railroad tycoon who died in 1916, was typical of the period: He was worth between $50 million and $100 million upon his death, equivalent to $2 billion or $3 billion today. In a period of no minimum wage, no environmental impact statements, and negligible or nonexistent income taxes, such fortunes were not uncommon.

Laissez-faire capitalism predated Darwin, but economists and others who supported the concept found much to like about social Darwinism. In a sense, social Darwinism justified the widespread use of laissez-faire economics. Because evolutionary theory, when applied to individual people, suggested that some human beings were better suited for economic competition than others, it stood to reason that those endowed with the greatest advantages would amass huge fortunes. Social Darwinism, then, lent a veneer of science to the argument for laissez-faire capitalism. Though the laissez-faire model was popular in American thought and politics before *On the Origin of Species* was published, the supposedly scientific argument drawn from social Darwinism certainly did not diminish the appeal of this economic system for Americans.

Social Darwinism also had a lot to say about race. In Darwin's time and for many years afterward, nearly all white Americans and Europeans were convinced that people of other races were inferior to them. European civilization, white people agreed, was clearly superior to anything that Africans, aboriginal Australians, or the native peoples of North and South America had managed to create. For years white Europeans and Americans had used this notion of racial superiority to justify their mistreatment of people with different skin tones. White people occupied the lands belonging to nonwhite peoples, seized the minerals and other resources those lands produced, and all too often enslaved, impoverished, or murdered the people who lived there.

Social Darwinism's Critics

Social Darwinism did not appeal to everyone. Many social reformers, in particular, opposed almost everything that social Darwinism stood for. In their eyes, people who achieved financial success did so not because they were somehow the "best," but for other reasons. One of these was luck; most members of the ruling classes had been fortunate enough to be born into an already well-off and well-connected family. Another reason was the legal system, which in both Europe and in the United States tended to favor those with more money at the expense of those with less. As the reformers saw it, then, it was untrue to say that the wealthy got ahead just because they were better or more deserving than everyone else.

Moreover, some observers worried that social Darwinism lacked a moral center. People routinely cheated one another in business dealings, for example, and nations often attacked other countries with little provocation. For many people these scenarios violated some sort of ethical code, but social Darwinism appeared to approve of such behavior. Whatever people did to get ahead, social Darwinists suggested, was acceptable: These actions stemmed from a natural desire to succeed, so no one should complain. Darwin, in fact, was among those who found this attitude distasteful. The world, he suggested, required compassion and cooperation as well as competition, and to ignore what was right in favor of what produced success was, in his opinion, wrong.

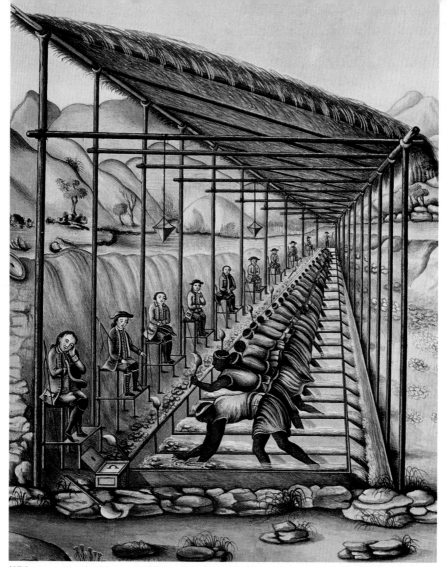

With overseers looking on, African slaves wash diamonds in Brazil. Social Darwinism played into already existing notions of white superiority over nonwhite peoples.

Social Darwinism did not generally change the way people in power thought about what they were doing with regard to race, but just as with laissez-faire capitalism, it offered these people an apparently scientific framework to support their racist ideas. In several obvious ways, from wealth to military power, countries like the United States and England had an enormous advantage over the cultures of most other parts of the globe. According to the way social Darwinists interpreted evolutionary theory, it was perfectly acceptable for more "advanced" civilizations to conquer those that were less well developed. Exactly as a stronger species would inevitably displace a weaker one in the wild, the better-equipped Americans and Europeans would defeat cultures possessing fewer advantages. "Theirs is a child race,"[32] one white American wrote dismissively about people of African descent. Social Darwinism thus provided a justification of sorts for the transgressions of white Americans and Europeans. The support social Darwinists gave to racial prejudice did nothing to help alleviate it.

Evolution and the Poor

What to do about the poor became another political question that social Darwinism attempted to answer. Social welfare systems in the years around 1900 were rudimentary by modern standards. Orphans, the chronically ill, and the disabled might get basic care in a community poorhouse or orphanage; the accommodations were far from luxurious, but they were probably better than the streets. Many communities also sponsored workhouses, where able-bodied indigents might stay in exchange for doing menial labor. These institutions, along with private charity offered by individuals, churches, and other organizations, typically served to keep the poor alive, if not exactly thriving.

From a strictly evolutionary standpoint, however, that assistance—minimal though it was—proved problematic. In nature, after all, the weakest individuals quickly died off, along with their genes. In the long run, the loss of these poorly equipped individuals and their genes strengthened the overall gene pool of the species. Yet the simple safety net of the era kept the most marginal people alive and allowed them to reproduce, and viewed from a social Darwinist perspective, that made no sense. "The weak members of civilized societies propagate their kind," summed up Darwin. "This must be highly injurious to the race of man." Noting that farmers select their strongest, healthiest animals for breeding purposes, Darwin pointed out that government policy regarding poor people was very different. "Excepting in the case of man himself," Darwin mused, "hardly anyone is so ignorant as to allow his worst animals to breed."[33]

The obvious answer to this conundrum was to withdraw support for the poor altogether, letting them starve to death and removing their genes from the gene pool, but few Americans or Europeans of the post-Darwin period were willing to go this far. The fictional miser Ebenezer Scrooge, the lead character in Charles Dickens's novel *A Christmas Carol*, may have wanted the poor in England to die off so as to "decrease the surplus population,"[34] but not many real Englishmen—or real Americans—were comfortable with this proposal. Darwin himself, though quite willing to admit that Britain's gene pool might be improved without its poorest citizens, nevertheless opposed eliminating aid to the poor. To do so, he explained, would be inhuman. "Nor could we check our sympathy [for the poor], even at the urging of hard reason," he wrote, "without deterioration in the noblest part of our nature."[35]

Eugenics

But even if there was little support for simply letting the poor die off, many social Darwinists were willing to take other measures to prevent the gene pool from being weakened. Among these was Darwin's cousin Francis Galton. A scientist and statistician, Galton believed that the "undesirables" in society—the poor, the chronically ill, and the developmentally disabled—should be steered away from having children and perhaps prevented from reproducing altogether. At the same time, he encouraged wealthier couples to have more children, to increase the number of people with more desirable characteristics. Known as eugenics, a word that literally means "well born," Galton's ideas for improving the quality of the gene pool proved popular both in Europe and America. Like many of those those who championed laissez-faire economics, eugenicists were sure that their ideas were grounded in Darwin's evolutionary theory. "What nature does blindly, slowly, and ruthlessly," Galton wrote, "man may do providentially [in a beneficial way], quickly, and kindly."[36]

Eugenics was most influential in the early 1900s. Between 1907 and 1921 over half of the American states passed laws banning reproduction among certain groups of people, most notably those with mental illness and those who had very low IQ scores. During the 1920s

WORDS IN CONTEXT

eugenics

The branch of study dedicated to improving the gene pool.

Rags to Riches

Not all poor people of the late 1800s and early 1900s were doomed to remain that way. Andrew Carnegie, for example, emigrated from Scotland to the United States with his desperately poor parents and eventually became one of the wealthiest men alive; James J. Hill, though not as poor as Carnegie, was certainly not well off as a youth. Many Americans were intrigued by the so-called rags-to-riches stories of these men and others like them, and fictional accounts of boys who worked their way up from poverty were enormously popular at the time.

Social Darwinists were happy to acknowledge that rags-to-riches stories were possible. Stories of people like Carnegie and Hill seemed to validate the truth of their beliefs: While the wealthy were more likely to be equipped for success, genes could be unpredictable. So despite his station in life, a poor boy might be born with the intelligence, drive, and acquisitiveness necessary for him to get ahead. To social Darwinists, this indicated the flexibility of their perspective—and again, as they saw it, reflected the way evolution worked in biology.

In fact, from the perspective of a social Darwinist, rags-to-riches tales indicated the great power of evolution in human societies. If a man like Carnegie, born with nothing, could meet with such obvious and overwhelming success, then the genes he was born with must have been potent indeed.

and 1930s, moreover, doctors forcibly sterilized tens of thousands of Americans, mainly lower-income women who were residents of asylums and other institutions. For the most part, Americans approved; a 1937 survey revealed that about two-thirds of the population supported sterilization as a means of increasing the quality of the gene pool. The notion that some people were "unfit" to have children can be traced directly to Galton—and to a degree, before him to Spencer. Eugenics, then, was very much a product of social Darwinism.

The widespread appeal of eugenics, however, did not last. In 1933 Adolf Hitler's Nazi Party took control of Germany. Influenced mainly by old antagonisms toward ethnic minorities and others, but also influenced in part by what it viewed as the success of eugenicist programs in California and elsewhere in the United States, the new government of Germany embarked on a massive program in which tens of thousands of people were forcibly sterilized. The Nazis soon became even more infamous for the unspeakable horrors of the Holocaust, during which they systematically murdered millions of people—Jews, Slavs, gypsies, the developmentally delayed, and many others—whose only crime was to carry genes that the Nazis believed were undesirable. The world was quite properly revulsed by the Holocaust, and as a result eugenics lost a good deal of support.

Thousands of bodies await burial at a Nazi concentration camp in 1945. Adolf Hitler and the Nazis took the idea of eugenics to a new level, murdering millions of people they deemed inferior and unworthy of life.

Today, social Darwinism no longer plays much of a role in economic, social, and political debate. No reputable politician or academic advocates the involuntary sterilization of the poor or supports policies that assume, for example, that African Americans are inferior to whites. Laissez-faire capitalism did not survive past the Great Depression and the New Deal of the 1930s, and the great majority of economists today have no interest in seeing it return. Still, the ideas of thinkers like Galton and Spencer were deeply influential for many years after Darwin's works were published, and as the example of eugenics demonstrates, in at least some cases they played an important role in debate about government policies. Without the theory of evolution, it is possible that these debates would have been very different.

CHAPTER FIVE

Evolution and
the Future

In 1785 James Hutton, one of the first scientists to speculate that Earth was a good deal older than the Bible suggested, gave a talk to a group of scholars. Though Hutton was not generally known for his eloquence, his speech that day included a phrase that has been frequently quoted in scientific circles and even beyond. In geology, Hutton explained, there was "no vestige of a beginning,—no prospect of an end."[37] As he saw it, the origins of the world lay so far back in time that no one could truly comprehend the number of years that had passed since its creation. Moreover, Hutton believed, the world would continue to exist for an indeterminate number of years; there was no way to guess how many.

Hutton, of course, was not speaking directly about evolution. He died more than a decade before Darwin was born, and his most famous works appeared well over half a century before *On the Origin of Species* was published. Nonetheless, Hutton's words resonate with biologists and others who study evolution. According to the best estimates of scientists today, life has existed on Earth for several billion years, long enough for evolution to have produced a mind-boggling variety of living things: spiders and amoebas, chimpanzees and chinchillas, microbes that live no more than ten minutes, and plants that flower only once a century. And with another two billion or more years stretching ahead of us—most estimates agree that Earth will remain hospitable to life for at least that long—there is no reason to suppose that evolution has reached a stopping point.

There is one possible exception, however, and that involves human beings. Some experts suggest that human evolution, unlike evolution elsewhere in the plant and animal kingdoms, may now be at an end. They point to recent changes in the way people live and travel and conclude that conditions of human life today are dramatically different from what they ever were in the past. Those changes, they argue, no longer allow further evolution. According to this perspective, while organisms from bacteria to redwoods will continue to undergo evolution just as they have for countless millennia, humans will not change appreciably. Genetically speaking, a person alive a million years from now—assuming, of course, that humanity survives that long—will be essentially the same as a person alive today.

Other experts, though, take up the opposite view. Not only will human evolution continue in the future, they argue, but the pace of evolutionary change will increase dramatically. For evidence they point to the world's growing knowledge of genetics along with technological innovations that are changing the way people live, work, and even think. In the opinion of these scientists, it will soon be possible for humans to guide their own evolution, strengthening the gene pool and making their descendants—in social Darwinist terms—ever better-equipped to survive, thrive, and reproduce. These two visions, one suggesting that human evolution is over, the other asserting that it will proceed more quickly than ever before, are obviously at odds with one another, but both have their supporters, and both make a certain amount of sense.

> **WORDS IN CONTEXT**
>
> *microbes*
> Small organisms that can cause disease.

The Effects of Isolation

One of Charles Darwin's first indications of evolutionary change came from his research on the Galapagos Islands. He discovered that many of the islands he visited had their own distinctive species of finch, birds distinguishable from one another mainly by the sizes and shapes of their beaks. Darwin reasoned that the finches had once all been the same species but had over time become isolated from one another. Instead of interbreeding with finches from other islands, they had produced offspring only with finches that already made their homes on the same island. Through mutation and natural selection, finches on different islands came to develop somewhat different sets of genes—enough to establish them as separate species.

Scientists estimate that life has existed on Earth for several billion years. During that enormous span of time, evolution has resulted in a mind-boggling variety of living things.

Darwin assumed that the finches had diverged so much in large part because of their geographic isolation, and he was quite correct. Because there was no intermixing of the birds, any genetic changes remained restricted to only one island, and after a sufficient number of years the finches had become separate species. Since Darwin's time, scientists have found many other situations in which islands, mountain ranges, rivers, and other geographic features have created barriers between two or more populations of a species, leading eventually to the establishment of a species that is entirely new. As anthropologist Ian Tattersall puts it, "Everything we know about evolutionary change suggests that genetic innovations are only likely to become fixed in small, isolated populations."[38] So common is this process that it has been given a name by evolutionary biologists: allopatric speciation.

For allopatric speciation to work, however, it is necessary for the two populations to remain isolated for thousands upon thousands of years. In theory, even a small amount of contact between two populations that are steadily diverging—but are not yet completely different species—could put an end to the process. A pair of finches making the trek from one island in the Galapagos chain to another, a few stray seeds from a plant blowing across a lake during a windstorm, a sudden cold spell that forces a group of small mammals to cross a mountain—any of these events could insert new genes into a population, slowing or stopping the divergence of two species and, in effect, resetting the evolutionary clock to zero. If evolution is to take place most efficiently, then, geographical barriers are required.

> **WORDS IN CONTEXT**
>
> *speciation*
> The development of new species from existing ones.

The End of Evolution?

But when many modern scientists look at human beings, they no longer see these barriers. In today's interconnected world, no population can remain isolated from the rest of humanity for long. To travel between any two large metropolitan areas anywhere in the world takes a day or two at the most. Sparsely inhabited Pacific islands are routinely visited in modern times by ships and airplanes, bringing visitors and new residents to the islands and taking people who already live there on trips to other parts of the world. Traditional communities in the Amazon basin and in the New Guinea highlands are no longer cut off from the bulk of the world as they were even fifty years ago. As movement increases, intermarriage will become more and more common. The result will be a remixing of genes and a halt to any development of new human species that may already be under way.

Tattersall is one of many experts who believe that the changes in the way people live have already put an end to evolution among humans.

Given the ease of travel and the increasing mixing of populations from distant spots on the globe, he argues, it is "highly improbable" that new mutations will ever again take hold within human populations. Tattersall is careful not to imply that a lack of mutations is a bad thing—or for that matter a good thing—but he is certain that the era of evolution, for humanity at least, is over. "Human beings," he concludes, "are just going to have to learn to live with themselves as they are."[39] Other scholars agree. Where evolution is concerned, says British professor Steve Jones, "things have simply stopped getting better, or worse, for our species."[40]

The lack of isolated populations is not the only reason some believe that human evolution may have reached its endpoint. Hearkening back to the social Darwinists of a hundred years ago and more, Jones points out that modern medicine and social welfare policies have lessened, if not eliminated, the likelihood of evolution in the future. Until quite recently in human history, people who were physically weak, developmentally disabled, or chronically ill often did not survive into adulthood. The result was that their genes were not passed on to the next generation. Today, that is no longer true. "Darwin's machine has lost its power," Jones argues, referring to Darwin's assertion that natural selection was the driving force behind evolutionary change. "The fact that everybody stays alive . . . means that [evolution has] got nothing to work with."[41]

Genetics and the Future

Jones and Tattersall represent a particular set of views on the future of human evolution. Their perspective, however, is by no means the only one reached by experts. Many other scholars strongly disagree with the conclusions of those who say that human evolution has come to an end. In their opinion evolution is still very much a part of the human future. A few of these theorists base their argument on history. Evolution, they point out, has always been a part of life on Earth, and there is no good reason to believe that things will change just because populations are no longer isolated or because people who once would have died in childhood now live to reproduce. "You simply cannot predict evolutionary events," cautions one scholar. "Who knows where we are headed?"[42]

Three young women enjoy a warm reception on their arrival in the highlands of Papua New Guinea. Many traditional communities there and elsewhere are no longer cut off from the rest of world.

Other opponents of the notion that human evolution is complete base their reasoning not on history but on genetics. Understanding of genetics is far greater today than it was just a generation or two ago. Scientists of the twenty-first century, for example, can often determine precisely what qualities or characteristics an individual gene controls. As a result, scientists can sometimes identify the traits an organism will carry simply by examining its genes. Since advances in technology have made analysis of genetic material both easier and cheaper than ever before, it is not difficult to imagine couples comparing their genetic profiles before agreeing to marry. If the combinations of their genes seem likely to produce the "best" possible children, the couple will probably go through with the wedding, whereas if one partner's genes are found wanting, the marriage might be called off.

One expert who believes that this scenario might become a reality in the near future is an American psychologist named Geoffrey Miller. As selection of mates based on genetics increases, Miller predicts "a rise in average physical attractiveness and health." If more babies

Humans and Speciation

As Darwin realized when he studied the finches of the Galapagos, isolation is important for evolution. But isolation must continue for an extended period of time for mutations and natural selection to have their effect. Although some populations of human beings remained quite isolated until relatively recently, they had not been on their own nearly long enough to form an entirely new species. Probably no group was isolated from the rest of the world for more than about fifty thousand years—an eternity compared to a human life span, but not enough for evolution to work. No one argues, then, that humans were just about to split into new species until recent innovations in travel stopped that process.

Nonetheless, over many thousands of years some genetic traits have become closely linked to certain populations. Human blood, for example, is often classified into four basic types: A, AB, B, and O. These types appear to have little if any evolutionary advantage, but they are nonetheless passed on as a part of an individual's genetic material. The four types, however, are not distributed evenly across the world. Type A blood, for example, was common among Europeans and the aborigines of Australia—but altogether absent among the native peoples of South America. Over the years, it seems, the gene associated with type A blood had been eliminated from that population. It is not difficult to see how, given sufficient time and enough small and unimportant changes like this one, isolated peoples might someday have developed into separate species.

with these desirable characteristics are born, the gene pool will slowly change to favor those traits. In addition, Miller says, "you will probably get selection for physical traits that tend to be attractive in both males and females—things like height, muscularity, [and] energy levels."[43] Given time, the emphasis on these traits will change the way humankind looks and acts. And if genetic technologies are available mainly to the well off, as they typically are today, significant differences in health, intellectual abilities, and other areas might eventually develop between rich and poor.

Genetic manipulation is also a possibility in the future. Suppose that a child is born with a gene that its parents would prefer their baby did not have—a gene that predisposes the child to a serious disease, for instance, or that threatens to make success in school difficult or even impossible. At some point it may be feasible to replace these unwanted genes with other genes that are more desirable. Perhaps in this way the average human life span could be gradually extended to 125 years or even 150. Or the goal might be somewhat more modest: "Our genome [genetic profile] could be tweaked to make future generations resistant to HIV,"[44] points out one commentator. If this sort of tweaking of genes proves workable, it could completely change some of the limitations humans have been living with since the beginning of time. That would lead, in turn, to enormous differences in how people of the future live their lives.

Other Scenarios

Using genetics to double human life spans may sound like the stuff of the distant future, but people like Miller believe we are on our way to making that a reality. More far-fetched, perhaps, are the ideas of people who agree with Miller that further human evolution is inevitable, but suggest that it will take place in completely new and potentially unexpected ways. American anthropologist John Hawks, for example, has speculated that space travel—and the settling of humans in isolated space colonies—could result in a new wave of evolution among people. "If we had spacefaring people who went on one-way voyages to distant stars," Hawks theorizes, "that might be enough to trigger speciation."[45] True, Hawks concedes, the new colonies would have to remain apart from populations still on Earth for tens of thousands of years, perhaps more. But as technology improves, the idea is perhaps not completely out of the question.

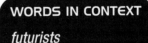

WORDS IN CONTEXT

futurists

People who study what the future may be like.

And other theorists look to the steady increase in artificial intelligence for clues about how human evolution could proceed. Someday, a few futurists believe, humans will be able to "upload" themselves—that is, to produce electronic copies of their brains and perhaps of their bodies as well. "Evolutionary selection could occur in a population of uploads or artificial intelligence just as

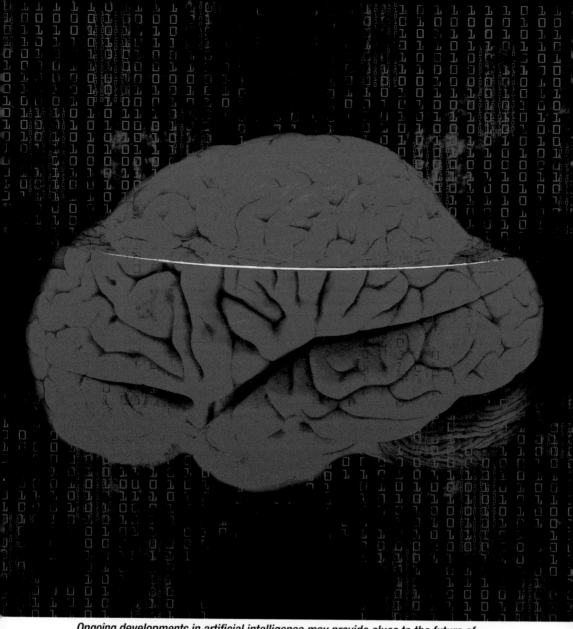

Ongoing developments in artificial intelligence may provide clues to the future of human evolution. Some futurists believe that humans will someday be able to upload themselves, producing electronic copies of their brains.

much as it could in a population of biological organisms,"[46] explains futurist Nick Bostrom of the United Kingdom. In fact, Bostrom argues, the pace of evolutionary change would likely increase because uploaded humans could reproduce much more quickly than flesh-and-blood humans can. Where ordinary people might produce four or five distinct generations in a century, for example, electronic brains might be able to manage a hundred thousand generations in the same time span—more than enough to allow for clear evolutionary changes.

Of course, whether the uploaded humans Bostrom describes count as "people" or not is another question entirely, and even Bostrom admits that we are probably many years away from storing our brains on a server. Nonetheless, Bostrom's argument—and Hawks's suggestion of space colonies—can serve as a reminder that much about human evolution in the future remains completely uncertain. Perhaps, as some argue, evolution truly is dead, and humanity will stay just as it

Physical Changes

Throughout history humans have undergone dramatic changes in their physical appearance. Human teeth, for example, have steadily become smaller; our ancestors who lived approximately one hundred thousand years ago had teeth considerably larger than those of people who live today. Toes, similarly, have gotten shorter and generally less useful as humans have moved down from the trees and become adapted to life on flatter ground. Not everything has shrunk, however; humans are much taller than they used to be, and the size of human skulls has increased as the human brain has grown bigger.

Most of these trends will likely continue. Indeed, some evolutionists argue that the little toe, the most useless of the five, will someday disappear altogether. Height, similarly, may well continue to increase as nutrition improves. But opinions about skull size and the future are divided. Some argue that the human skull has reached its greatest possible size. Any larger, and mothers would have difficulty pushing their babies out of the womb. Evolution, then, will not permit humans to develop skulls any larger than those of today.

But others look at modern medicine and come to a different conclusion. More and more children, after all, are being born via caesarean section; they are lifted into the world through the miracle of surgery. Perhaps someday that will be the normal way of giving birth. In that case, there may be no limit on the size of the human skull in the future.

currently is for as long as people continue to roam the world. Perhaps, as others believe, we are the masters of our fates, able someday to use genetics to control how—and in what direction—evolution will proceed from here to the end of our time on Earth. Or perhaps, none of these thinkers are right, and human evolution will remain what it always has been: a force to be reckoned with and a power that cannot be controlled, taking humans wherever it may happen to lead them. Only time will tell.

SOURCE NOTES

Introduction: Evolution and Society

1. Norman D. Newell, *Creation and Evolution*. New York: Praeger, 1985, p. 4.
2. Quoted in Kenneth R. Miller, *Only a Theory*. New York: Viking, 2008, p. 2.

Chapter One: Before Darwin

3. Carl Degler, *In Search of Human Nature*. New York: Oxford University Press, 1991, p. 5.
4. Quoted in Loren Eiseley, *Darwin's Century*. Garden City, NY: Doubleday, 1958, p. 30.
5. Degler, *In Search of Human Nature*, p. 5.
6. Eiseley, *Darwin's Century*, p. 8.
7. Quoted in Carl Zimmer, *Evolution: The Triumph of an Idea*. New York: HarperCollins, 2001, p. 10.
8. Quoted in Zimmer, *Evolution: The Triumph of an Idea*, p. 12.

Chapter Two: A New Idea

9. Quoted in Randy Moore, Mark Decker, and Sehoya Cotner, *Chronology of the Evolution-Creationism Controversy*. Santa Barbara, CA: ABC-CLIO, 2010, p. 39.
10. Quoted in Zimmer, *Evolution: The Triumph of an Idea*, p. 13.
11. Zimmer, *Evolution: The Triumph of an Idea*, p. 15.
12. Quoted in Eiseley, *Darwin's Century*, p. 150.
13. Quoted in Moore, Decker, and Cotner, *Chronology of the Evolution-Creationism Controversy*, p. 47.
14. Quoted in Eiseley, *Darwin's Century*, p. 148.
15. Quoted in Eiseley, *Darwin's Century*, p. 171.
16. Zimmer, *Evolution: The Triumph of an Idea*, p. 35.
17. Quoted in Zimmer, *Evolution: The Triumph of an Idea*, p. 48.
18. Quoted in Edward J. Larson, *Summer for the Gods*. Cambridge, MA: Harvard, 1997, p. 17.
19. Quoted in Zimmer, *Evolution: The Triumph of an Idea*, p. 46.

Chapter Three: Backlash

20. Quoted in Larson, *Summer for the Gods*, p. 17.
21. Quoted in Randy Moore, *Dinosaurs by the Decades*. Santa Barbara, CA: ABC-CLIO, 2014, p. 166.
22. Quoted in Darwin Project, "Sedgwick, Adam, to Darwin, C.R.," entry 2548, Darwin Correspondence Database. www.darwinproject.ac.uk.
23. Zimmer, *Evolution: The Triumph of an Idea*, p. 51.
24. Quoted in Larson, *Summer for the Gods*, p. 39.
25. Quoted in Miller, *Only a Theory*, p. 228.
26. Quoted in Larson, *Summer for the Gods*, p. 189.
27. Quoted in Larson, *Summer for the Gods*, p. 190.
28. Quoted in Brian J. Alters and Sandra M. Alters, *Defending Evolution*. Sudbury, MA: Jones and Bartlett, 2001, p. 37.

Chapter Four: Social Darwinism

29. Quoted in PBS, *American Experience*, "People and Events: Herbert Spencer," 1999. www.pbs.org.
30. Daniel Kevles, *In the Name of Eugenics*. Cambridge, MA: Harvard, 1995, p. ix.
31. Quoted in PBS, *American Experience*, "People and Events: Herbert Spencer."
32. Quoted in Robert C. Bannister, *Social Darwinism*. Philadelphia: Temple, 1979, p. 196.
33. Quoted in Bannister, *Social Darwinism*, p. 30.
34. Charles Dickens, *A Christmas Carol*. London: Bradbury & Evans, 1858, p. 9.
35. Quoted in Bannister, *Social Darwinism*, p. 30.
36. Francis Galton, "Eugenics: Its Definition, Scope, and Aims," *American Journal of Sociology*, vol. X, no. 1, July 1904. http://galton.org.

Chapter Five: Evolution and the Future

37. Quoted in Eiseley, *Darwin's Century*, p. 73.
38. Quoted in James Owen, "Future Humans: Four Ways We May, or May Not, Evolve," *National Geographic News*, November 24, 2009. http://news.nationalgeographic.com.

39. Quoted in Owen, "Future Humans."
40. Quoted in Robin McKie, "Is Human Evolution Finally Over?," *Guardian*, February 3, 2002. www.theguardian.com.
41. Quoted in Owen, "Future Humans."
42. Quoted in McKie, "Is Human Evolution Finally Over?"
43. Quoted in Owen, "Future Humans."
44. James Kingsland, "Do We Have the Right to Shape Human Evolution, Wonders Robert Winston," *Guardian*, July 1, 2014. www.theguardian.com.
45. Quoted in Owen, "Future Humans."
46. Quoted in Owen, "Future Humans."

IMPORTANT PEOPLE IN THE HISTORY OF EVOLUTION THEORY

William Jennings Bryan was an American orator, lawyer, and politician. He argued against the possibility of evolution during the Scopes Trial in 1925 and was attacked by attorney Clarence Darrow for his views on the inerrancy of the Bible.

Charles Darwin is generally recognized as the first person who understood how evolution took place. He is usually credited with developing the idea of natural selection, and his two books, *On the Origin of Species* and *The Descent of Man*, were enormously influential.

Francis Galton, a cousin of Darwin's, was the founder of eugenics. A British scientist, Galton advocated improving the gene pool, most notably by encouraging well-off people to have more children than the poor.

Thomas Huxley was a British scientist who first denied the possibility of evolution but then came to support it. He enthusiastically defended Darwin's ideas against skeptical members of the public, including religious figures and other scientists alike.

Jean-Baptiste Lamarck was a French scientist who developed one of the earliest theories of evolution. He believed that species changed because of a nervous fluid that produced desirable physical changes in individuals of a given species, changes which then were passed on to later generations.

Herbert Spencer was perhaps the first to link Darwin's theories directly to the realm of human society, thus setting social Darwinist ideas into motion. He was the originator of the phrase "survival of the fittest."

Alfred Russel Wallace was a British scientist who independently came up with the idea of natural selection around the same time that Darwin developed it. He was a strong supporter of evolutionary theory when Darwin's works came under attack.

FOR FURTHER RESEARCH

Books

Sandra Herbert, *Charles Darwin and the Question of Evolution: A Brief History with Documents*. New York: Bedford, 2011.

Lauri Lebo, *The Devil in Dover: An Insider's Story of Dogma v. Darwin in Small-Town America*. New York: New Press, 2009.

Randy Moore, Mark Decker, and Sehoya Cotner, *Chronology of the Evolution-Creationism Controversy*. Santa Barbara, CA: ABC-CLIO, 2010.

Rebecca Stott, *Darwin's Ghosts: The Secret History of Evolution*. New York: Spiegel & Grau, 2012.

Ian Tattersall, *Masters of the Planet: The Search for Our Human Origins*. New York: Palgrave Macmillan, 2012.

Ian Tattersall and Rob deSalle, *The Great Human Journey: Around the World in 22 Million Days*. Boston: Bunker Hill, 2013.

Internet Sources

Robin McKie, "Is Human Evolution Finally Over?," *Guardian*, February 3, 2002. www.theguardian.com/science/2002/feb/03/genetics.research.

Dennis O'Neill, "Darwin and Natural Selection." http://anthro.palomar.edu/evolve/evolve_2.htm.

James Owen, "Future Humans: Four Ways We May, or May Not, Evolve," *National Geographic News*, November 24, 2009. http://news.nationalgeographic.com/news/2009/11/091124-origin-of-species-150-darwin-human-evolution.html.

Websites

American Museum of Natural History, "Darwin" (www.amnh.org /exhibitions/past-exhibitions/darwin). Information related to a museum exhibit about Darwin and evolutionary theory, including Darwin's life, objections to Darwin's ideas, a discussion of social Darwinism, and more.

NOVA, "Evolution" (www.pbs.org/wgbh/nova/evolution). A companion website to a video about evolution. Includes historical information about the development of evolutionary theory in addition to information about the workings of evolution.

PBS, "Evolution" (www.pbs.org/wgbh/evolution/index.html). About the process of evolution, including information on natural selection, Darwin, and the evolution of humans.

INDEX

impact of, 15–16
  science and, 15–22, 35–36
reproductive laws, 54–55
rich, the, 49, 50, 51, 64
Rockefeller, John D., 50

Satan, 18
schools
  creation science in, 43
  evolution in, 39–45
  intelligent design in, 43–45
science
  evolution and, 9–11
  history of, 12–15
  religion and, 15–22, 35–36
scientific evidence, 9–11, 13–15,
  20–22, 39
Scopes, John, 39–40
Scopes trial, 40–41
Sedgwick, Adam, 22, 26, 36
skull size, 67
social Darwinism, 11, 46–57, 62
social reformers, 51
social welfare, 53–54, 62
space travel, 65
speciation, 61, 64
species
  formation of new, 9, 59–61
  variations in, 24, 29
Spencer, Herbert, 47–49, 55

spontaneous generation, 12
sterilization, forced, 54–55, 57
survival of the fittest, 47–49

Tattersall, Ian, 60–61, 61–62
technology, 59, 63–65
teeth, 67
Ten Commandments, 38
theory
  definition of, 11
  See also evolutionary theory
toes, 67
traits
  passing down of, 30
  selection for specific, 63–64
type A blood, 64

universe, age of, 35, 58

variations, 24, 29

Wallace, Alfred Russel, 32, 33,
  34
wealthy people, 49, 50, 51, 55, 64
Wegener, Alfred, 34
Wells, William Charles, 24, 25
white superiority, 50–53
workhouses, 53

Zimmer, Carl, 25, 30, 38

PICTURE CREDITS

ABOUT THE AUTHOR

Stephen Currie is the author of many books and educational materials, including *Goblins*, *Hydropower*, and *The Panama Canal* for ReferencePoint Press. He has also taught at levels ranging from kindergarten to college. He lives with his family near the Hudson River in New York State.